BASKETBALL GREATS

Written by Paul Stevenson

CONTENTS

Tip-Off!	4
How It Started	6
The NBA and WNBA	8
Around the World	10
Michael Jordan	12
Rivals	14
Globetrotters	16
Kobe and Shaq	18
WNBA Slam Dunkers	20
Leading the League	22
Going for Gold	24
Basketball Giants	26
Top of the Game	28
All-Time Greats: Fun Facts	30
Glossary	31
Index	32

First published in 2024 by
Hungry Tomato Ltd
F15, Old Bakery Studios,
Blewetts Wharf, Malpas Road,
Truro, Cornwall,
TR1 1QH, UK.

Thanks to our editor, Julie Tofflemire.

Copyright © 2024 Hungry Tomato Ltd

No part of this publication may be reproduced, stored in a retrieval system, or transmitted in any form or by any means, electronic, mechanical, photocopying, recording, or otherwise, without prior written permission of the copyright owner.

A CIP catalogue record for this book is available from the British Library.

ISBN 9781835691175
Printed in China

Discover more at
www.hungrytomato.com

Neither the publisher nor the author shall be liable for any bodily harm or damage to property whatsoever that may caused as a result of conducting any of the activites in this book.

DISCLAIMER:
The moves and stunts featured in this book have been performed by experienced, highly-trained basketball players. Do not, under any circumstances, try them yourself.

All words in **BOLD** can be found in the glossary.

TIP-OFF!

Basketball is one of the most popular and exciting sports in the world.

You can **slam dunk** it.

You can shoot a **three-pointer**.

You can make the perfect pass to a teammate.

It's the only place where **stealing** is a good thing.

And you don't have to be tall to play... **BUT IT HELPS!**

Centre Victor Wembanyama is 2.24 metres tall!

HOW IT STARTED

Basketball was invented in the USA in 1891. It was invented by a Canadian sports teacher named Dr. James Naismith.

Naismith wanted to find an indoor game that his football team could play in the winter to keep fit.

The game was played with baskets that were used for carrying peaches. Each team had nine players.

There was no **shot clock**, so players took a long time to shoot. The first game ended 1-0.

Dr. James Naismith stands between two peach baskets.

Statue of Dr. James Naismith

Over time, the rules changed. Basketball became popular across the world.

BASKETBALL RULES:
- Five players per team.
- Games last 40 or 48 minutes.
- A basket is worth one, two or three points, depending on where the shot is taken.
- **Foul** too many times – you're out of the game!

THE NBA AND WNBA

The National Basketball Association (NBA) is the most famous league in the world.

The NBA has 29 teams in the USA and one in Canada.

Each team plays 82 games in the regular **season**.
The best 16 teams qualify for the **playoffs**.

The team that wins the playoffs is the NBA champion!

NBA Championship trophy

The first WNBA (Women's National Basketball Association) league game was played in 1997. The WNBA is made up of 12 teams in the USA.

The WNBA playoffs include the top eight teams, and there are three rounds.

The popularity of the league has been growing steadily.

AROUND THE WORLD

In Europe, the best teams play in the EuroLeague. There are 18 teams, and the season runs from October to April.

As of 2023, the most successful team in the league is Real Madrid. They have won eleven titles!

Walter Tavares of Real Madrid towers over EA7 Emporio Armani Milan players in a 2024 EuroLeague game.

Many countries have their own leagues. In Europe, the ACB League of Spain and the Greek Basket League (GBL) of Greece have fierce competition.

The **top-tier** league in Australia is the National Basketball League (NBL). In China, the best players compete in the Chinese Basketball Association (CBA).

An ACB League match between FC Barcelona and Real Madrid

MICHAEL JORDAN

Michael Jordan is probably the best basketball player in history.

He played for the Chicago Bulls for 13 seasons and won six NBA titles.

> "Some people want it to happen, some wish it would happen, others make it happen." - **Michael Jordan**

Michael Jordan

Jordan's nickname was "Air Jordan". He could jump so high that it looked like he was flying through the air!

Jordan was the NBA **Rookie** of the Year in 1985, and he was named the "Most Valuable Player of the NBA" five times. Jordan retired in 2003.

Michael Jordan

JORDAN WAS ALSO AN EXCELLENT DEFENDER!

RIVALS

When two teams or two players really want to beat each other every time they meet, they're rivals!

One of the biggest rivalries in basketball is between the Boston Celtics and the Los Angeles Lakers. They've met in the NBA Finals 12 times!

Magic Johnson of the Lakers and Larry Bird of the Celtics were huge rivals in the 1980s.

The rivalry started when the two were playing college basketball. They faced each other in the 1979 NCAA Division I Championship. When they were opponents again in the NBA... it was game on!

"The first thing I would do every morning was look at the box scores to see what Magic did. I didn't care about anything else." - **Larry Bird**

NBA TITLES
- Magic Johnson: 5
- Larry Bird: 3

GLOBETROTTERS

The Harlem Globetrotters are a special team who mix awesome basketball skills with making crowds laugh!

The Globetrotters were formed in 1926. They have visited over 120 countries.

THE GLOBETROTTERS ARE FAMOUS FOR THEIR TRICK SHOTS.

TRICK SHOTS:
- Spinning the ball on one finger
- Balancing a ball on the neck and then flipping it in
- Making half-court shots or even shots from the **stands**
- And don't forget the epic slam dunks!

From 1971 to 1995, the Globetrotters won 8,829 games in a row. They have won over 27,000 games, and they play 400+ games a year!

KOBE AND SHAQ

KOBE BRYANT

Bryant turned professional when he was 18 years old. At the time, he was the youngest NBA player ever.

In 2006, Bryant scored an incredible 81 points in one game!

Bryant spent 20 years with the Los Angeles Lakers and retired in 2016.

Kobe Bryant shoots a **free throw** for his 81st point.

Sadly, he died in a helicopter crash in 2020, but his legend lives on.

SHAQUILLE O'NEAL

Better known as "Shaq", O'Neal has won four NBA championships, three of them with Bryant.

Shaq was an agile player despite his size – he is 2.16 metres tall and weighed 180 kg in 2002!

Shaq was Rookie of the Year for the 1992–93 season. He scored over 28,000 points in his 19-year career.

Shaquille O'Neal

Kobe Bryant

WNBA SLAM DUNKERS

WNBA players Candace Parker and Lisa Leslie have something amazing in common. They are the first two women players to slam dunk in a WNBA game.

Candace Parker was Rookie of the Year in 2008 and the Defensive Player of the Year in 2020.

Parker can skillfully play any position on the floor, but most often, you'll find her as a centre or **forward**.

Candace Parker

Lisa Leslie won four Olympic gold medals, two WNBA titles and three "Most Valuable Player" awards.

Leslie retired in 2009 but still holds her record of all-time scorer for the Los Angeles Sparks, with 6,263 points.

Lisa Leslie doing a slam dunk

LEADING THE LEAGUE

Diana Taurasi and Sue Bird have been wowing WNBA fans for years, and setting records with their skills.

DIANA TAURASI

Taurasi is definitely one of the WNBA's greatest players. She is the all-time leading scorer of the WNBA, with over 10,000 points and counting.

She has won 3 WNBA titles and five Olympic gold medals.

Diana Taurasi plays for the Phoenix Mercury.

SUE BIRD

Bird played in more WNBA games than anyone else in league history!

She has four championship wins and is said to be the game's greatest **point guard**.

Bird was a dedicated team player. She even played with a broken nose! Bird retired in 2022.

GOING FOR GOLD

The US men's and women's teams have dominated the Olympic Games!

The US men's team has won 16 of the 20 Olympic men's tournaments.

For the women's team, it's 9 of the 12 tournaments, with a winning streak of 7 gold medals in a row!

Kevin Durant contributed to three of the team's gold-medal wins. He is also a four-time NBA scoring champion.

Kevin Durant

The most famous US Olympic team was the 1992 "Dream Team" (see above). It featured Michael Jordan, Magic Johnson, Larry Bird, John Stockton and Karl Malone. In one game, they beat Angola by 68 points!

Tina Charles is a three-time gold medalist. She is the all-time leader in **rebounds** for New York Liberty, with 1,243.

Tina Charles

BASKETBALL GIANTS

There's no denying that height plays a big role in basketball. Some players are considered giants even to their tall teammates.

Yao Ming from China is one of the most famous players in the world. He is 2.29 metres tall.

Ming spent his eight-year NBA career with the Houston Rockets, playing centre.

The tallest ever NBA player is Gheorghe Muresan from Romania.

GHEORGHE MURESAN IS AN AWESOME 2.31 METRES TALL!

The smallest NBA player ever is Muggsy Bogues. He is only 1.6 metres tall.

Muggsy Bogues

Gheorghe Muresan

"I always believed in myself. That's the attitude I took out on the floor – knowing that I belonged. That with my talents, my abilities, there's a place for me out there." - **Muggsy Bogues**

TOP OF THE GAME

Even among the top stars, Stephen Curry and LeBron James stand out!

Point guard Stephen Curry is the highest-paid player in the NBA. In 2021, he signed a four-year £170 million deal with the Golden State Warriors.

Curry also plays for the US men's national team.

STATS

NBA Championship: 4
NBA Most Valuable Player: 2
NBA Finals MVP: 1 (2022)

LeBron James is the all-time leading scorer in NBA history. He has over 48,000 regular season and playoffs points!

He has three Olympic medals – two gold and one bronze.

LeBron is a fan favourite. Each year, fans get to vote on who will play in the NBA's All-Star Game. LeBron has been selected 20 times – another record!

LeBron James

ALL-TIME GREATS: FUN FACTS

- Magic Johnson and Larry Bird are good friends now. They published a book together in 2020.

- Diana Taurasi has a nap before every game. Even if the game is at noon, she'll wake up, have a morning nap and then wake up again, ready for the game.

- Michael Jordan briefly left basketball in 1994 and played Major League Baseball professionally for one season. He returned to basketball in 1995 with a two-word press release – **"I'M BACK."**

GLOSSARY

centre – usually the tallest defender in the team. They are important for defense as well as offense.

forward – a strong player who plays close to the basket.

foul – called by the referee if the rules are broken.

free throw – a shot worth one point after a foul is called.

league – a group of teams who compete to win a championship. Each team plays all the others in the league at least once.

playoffs – the end-of-season competition.

point guard – the player whose job it is to bring the ball from one end of the court to the other.

professional – a player who is paid to play.

rebound – grabbing the ball after a shot is missed.

rookie – a player's first year in the league.

season – the period of time during which a league plays for a championship.

shot clock – a clock which shows the amount of time that a player has to take a shot.

slam dunk – jumping really high above the rim of the net and throwing the ball down through the hoop.

stands – the area in a sports stadium where people stand or sit to watch the game.

stealing – taking the ball away from an opponent.

three-pointer – a shot from long range which is worth three points.

top-tier – the highest level or rank.

INDEX

A
ACB League of Spain 11

B
Bird, Larry 14-15, 24, 30
Bird, Sue 22-23
Bogues, Muggsy 27
Boston Celtics 14
Bryant, Kobe 18-19

C
CBA (Chinese Basketball Association) 11
Charles, Tina 25
Chicago Bulls 12
Curry, Stephen 28

D
Dream Team 24
Durant, Kevin 24

E
Euroleague 10

G
GBL (Greek Basketball League) 11
Golden State Warriors 28

H
Houston Rockets 26

J
James, LeBron 28-29
Johnson, Magic 14-15, 24, 30
Jordan, Michael 12-13, 24, 30

L
Leslie, Lisa 20-21
Los Angeles Lakers 14, 18
Los Angeles Sparks 21

M
Malone, Karl 24
Ming, Yao 26
Muresan, Gheorghe 27

N
Naismith, Dr. James 6
NBA (National Basketball Association) 8, 12-13, 14-15, 18-19, 24, 26-27, 28-29
New York Liberty 25

O
O'Neal, Shaquille 18-19
Olympic basketball 21, 22, 24-25, 29

P
Parker, Candace 20
Phoenix Mercury 22
playoffs 8-9, 29, 31
point guards 23, 28, 31
points 7, 18-19, 21, 22, 24, 29

R
Real Madrid 10-11

S
slam dunks 4, 17, 20-21, 31
stealing 5, 31
Stockton, John 24

T
Taurasi, Diana 22, 30
The Harlem Globetrotters 6-17

W
Wembanyama, Victor 5
WNBA (Women's National Basketball Association) 8-9, 20-21, 22-23

Picture credits:
(t=top; b=bottom; m=middle; l=left; r=right):
AFP/Getty Images 27ml, 29bg. Dr. James Naismith Basketball Foundation, Almonte, Ontario, Canada: 6bl. Getty Images: 24b, 27mr. NBAE/Getty Images: 13bg, 15bg, 18b, 19b, 20bg, 21b, 26bg. Shutterstock: A.RICARDO 1bg, 24tr; Victor Velter 5tr; Art Babych 6br; Imtmphoto 7bg; Lev radin 8bl; Fabrizio Andrea Bertani 10bg; Christian Bertrand 11bg; CESM I Studio 14ml; Keeton Gale 17br, 22b, 31b; Ferenc Szelepcsenyi 17bl; Randy Miramontez 16bg; Dimitry Argunov 23b, 25bg; Photoyh 28bg; Below The Sky 30b; Michele Morrone 2-3bg; Alex Kravtsov 4-5bg; VectorArtist7 14mr; Taka1022 8-9bg. Sports Ollustrated/Getty Images: 12bg.

Every effort has been made to trace the copyright holders, and we apologise in advance for any unintentional omissions. We would be pleased to insert the appropriate acknowledgements in any subsequent edition of this publication.